THE
JEDI
MASTER'S
QUIZBOOK

425 COSMIC QUESTIONS & ANSWERS ABOUT
STAR WARS and *THE EMPIRE STRIKES BACK*

THE JEDI MASTER'S QUIZBOOK

425 COSMIC QUESTIONS & ANSWERS ABOUT *STAR WARS* and *THE EMPIRE STRIKES BACK*

RUSTY MILLER

DEL REY

A Del Rey Book
BALLANTINE BOOKS • NEW YORK

To my Mom and Dad,
and my dogs,
Frodo, Barney, and Puddy

FOREWORD

"A long time ago, in a galaxy far, far away . . ." These are the opening words of two of the most popular films ever made—*Star Wars* and *The Empire Strikes Back.*

This is a trivia book about those two films, with questions ranging from the obvious to the obscure. My editors at Lucasfilm have supplemented the book with some additional questions—although we tried to stay mainly with questions that can be answered from the movies, some are drawn from other sources. These questions are marked with an asterisk, and the materials used are the following:

The *Star Wars* and *Empire* novelizations
The Art of Star Wars and *The Art of Empire*
The Empire Strikes Back Notebook
The Star Wars Album
The Empire Collectors' Edition
The 1981 Empire Calendar

The Wookiee Storybook
Once Upon a Galaxy: The Making of Empire
The Star Wars Sketchbook
Bantha Tracks (the *Star Wars* fan-club news-
  letter)
The *Star Wars* and *Empire* soundtrack albums

I would like to thank in particular my good
friends, David Little, Chris Fortier, and Shawn
Meredith; my parents, Edward and Nancy Miller;
Lisa Kernan at Lucasfilm; and numerous other
friends and relatives. They all contributed to the
work necessary to make this book a success.

MAY THE FORCE BE WITH YOU!

Rusty Miller

STAR WARS QUESTIONS

1. What spaceport was the cantina in?

2. Where was Princess Leia from?

3. What was the name of the creature who worked for Jabba the Hutt and was shot by Han Solo?*

4. What vehicle did Luke drive on Tatooine?

5. What vehicle did the jawas drive?

6. What was Leia's starship called at the beginning of *Star Wars*?*

7. What were the names of Luke's two friends who had already entered the Academy?

8. What was the name of the freighter that Biggs Darklighter served on after graduating from the Academy?*

9. What was the vulnerable spot on the Death Star at which the Rebel fighters aimed?

10. What did Ben Kenobi do to scare the sand-people away from Luke's landspeeder?*

11. What was Threepio afraid would happen to him and Artoo if the Empire captured them on the Blockade Runner?

12. How did R2-D2 and C-3PO get away from the captured Rebel ship?

13. Why did Vader keep Leia's capture secret?

14. What order did Vader give that insured Leia's capture would remain secret?

15. How do we know when Artoo "comes to" inside the sandcrawler?

16. What clues found by the stormtroopers on the Tatooine desert first alerted them to the droids' presence?

17. What was Luke playing with while Threepio was taking his oil bath?

18. Where did Uncle Owen tell Luke he was planning to send the droids and for what purpose?

19. What kind of work did Luke and his uncle do?

20. What piece of machinery did they use in their work?

21. What creatures did the sandpeople ride?

22. What was Luke's original ambition before strange twists of fate made him a Rebel commander?

23. What were the names of the two suns of Tatooine?*

24. Who commanded the Rebel forces on the Yavin base?*

25. Who sold R2-D2 and C-3PO?

26. What was the name of the planet destroyed by the Death Star?

27. Who was Ben Kenobi's pupil long ago?

28. Who claimed that the Death Star was the ultimate power in the universe?

29. What was the most memorable feature of the alien who followed Luke and the others in Mos Eisley and then reported them to the stormtroopers?

30. How fast did Han claim that the Millennium Falcon could go?

31. What did Ben put on Luke's head when he was training him in the use of the Force?

32. Where, in her attempt to save Alderaan, did Leia say the main Rebel base was?

33. How many captured Rebels were marched down the hall by the stormtroopers?

34. What kind of mission did Leia insist that her ship was on?

35. How many stormtroopers captured Leia on the Blockade Runner?

36. Why did Jabba the Hutt put a price on Han Solo's head?

37. How many engines did Princess Leia's ship, the Blockade Runner, have?

38. What weapon did a Tusken Raider use?

39. Where did Luke get the rope that he and Leia used to swing over the chasm in the Death Star?

40. What made Vader's TIE fighter different from other fighters?

41. Why didn't the Empire shoot down Artoo and Threepio when they escaped from the Blockade Runner?

42. What was one of the tortures Grand Moff Tarkin and Darth Vader used to try to force information from Princess Leia?

43. What tool enabled Luke to see the battle between the Rebel Blockade Runner and the Star Destroyer?*

44. What was Threepio afraid that the jawas were going to do to him and Artoo?

45. Why did Uncle Owen order Luke to take Artoo to Anchorhead?

46. How many sandpeople raided Luke's landspeeder?

47. Who did Vader attack, using the Force, in the conference room on the Death Star?

48. Who ordered him to stop?

49. What did Luke and Ben do with the dead jawas?

50. How many Star Destroyers pursued the Falcon as it left Mos Eisley and Tatooine?

51. What did Chewbacca do to make the Falcon come out of hyperspace as it approached Alderaan?

52. How did Han and Chewie find the Death Star?

53. What was the seating capacity of a land-speeder?

54. What was the number of the Mos Eisley docking bay holding the Millennium Falcon?

55. What secret information was R2-D2 carrying in his memory bank?

56. Where was Ben Kenobi's home on Tatooine?

57. Who won the lightsaber duel between Darth Vader and Ben Kenobi?

58. Who killed Luke's Uncle Owen and Aunt Beru?

59. What was the name of the droid that Luke and his uncle first bought from the jawas, which, when it broke down, was replaced by R2-D2?*

60. Whose idea was it to blow up Alderaan?

61. What is another word used for the seeker?

62. Where did Luke, Han, Leia, and Chewbacca get trapped and almost killed?

63. What was all that was left of Ben after his lightsaber duel with Darth Vader?

64. When Darth Vader told Tarkin on the Death Star that "this will be a day long remembered," to what did he refer besides Ben's death?

65. What was Tarkin's title?

66. What was the name of Luke's best friend, who was slain in the battle of the Death Star?

67. What was the name of Biggs's friend, also slain in the battle of the Death Star?*

68. What color codes were given to the two squads of Rebel fighters attacking the Death Star?

69. What vehicle did Luke use on Tatooine besides the landspeeder?*

70. What was the unique power of the Death Star?

71. Which Rebel pilot made the first attempt to hit the Death Star target?

72. What three instructions did Luke give Artoo during the battle of the Death Star?

73. Who handed Leia the medals for Han and Luke on the Yavin base?

74. How did the Falcon's crew locate the tractor beam on the Death Star?

75. How was the Empire able to follow the Falcon to the Rebel base?

76. What did Luke compare hitting the Death Star target to?

77. How did Han endanger all their lives in the trash compacter?

78. Where was the Rebel base located?

79. What forced the Falcon to land on the Death Star?

80. What disguise did Luke and Han wear on the Death Star?

81. How many spikes did a Tusken Raider have on top of his head?

82. Which X-wing pilot destroyed the Death Star?

83. How did jawas load droids aboard the sand-crawlers?*

84. What was the number of the cell block in which Leia was held on the Death Star?

85. What evidence did Vader have that Leia and the Blockade Runner were not on a diplomatic mission?

86. What did Threepio say was his first job?

87. What was wrong with the red R2 unit that caused Uncle Owen and Luke to select Artoo instead?

88. Who did Threepio give thanks to when he was about to take his oil bath?

89. What made Luke think Artoo and Threepio had seen a lot of action when he was cleaning them up for Uncle Owen?

90. What did Artoo say was responsible for short-circuiting his recording system?

91. Who referred to Ben Kenobi as a wizard?

92. What did Luke think his father had done for a living before Ben Kenobi told him the truth?

93. What was the shape of the conference room on the Death Star?

94. When Tarkin announced that the Imperial Senate had been dissolved, who did he say would maintain control at the regional level?

95. What did Darth Vader do to Ben's cloak after he struck him down?

96. Where did Luke tell his uncle he was going to pick up some power converters?

97. How did Grand Moff Tarkin die?

98. What was General Tagge in charge of?*

99. What was Admiral Motti in charge of?*

100. What was the name of Leia's father?*

101. What happened to the band of jawas that sold Artoo and Threepio to Luke?

102. What do moisture vaporators do?*

103. Who gave Luke his lightsaber?

104. Who did Leia say would be able to retrieve the information Artoo carried once Ben delivered him to Alderaan?

105. What mechanism on the Falcon did Han use to get the coordinates for the jump to hyperspace?

106. When the Falcon was pulled into the Death Star, why did the Imperials believe there was no one on board?

107. According to Threepio, in how many locations was the tractor beam coupled to the Death Star's main reactor?

108. What was Vader's plan for the captured Rebel Blockade Runner?

109. What was Ben Kenobi's mission on the Death Star?

110. What did R2-D2 call C-3PO when the larger droid refused to get into the escape pod?

111. Who led the Rebels' strategy meeting for the Death Star attack?

112. What happened when the squad of storm-troopers found Leia on the Blockade Runner?

113. What did Luke ask Leia to do just before they swung across the chasm on the Death Star?

114. How did General Dodonna describe the fire power of the Death Star?

115. How many Rebel ships did the Imperial troops count making the assault on the Death Star?

116. What was Luke's Uncle Owen's last name?*

117. What language was Threepio required to speak for Uncle Owen?

118. How did Leia first appear to Luke?

119. What was the name of the place where the Tusken Raiders ambushed Luke?

120. What was Leia's father's title?*

121. How many monetary units did Ben Kenobi propose to pay Han for the trip to Alderaan?

122. What did the Empire find on Dantooine?

123. What was the number of Leia's cell on the Death Star?

124. What weapons did the Rebel fighters use to penetrate the Death Star's defenses?

125. Where did Luke and Han first meet?

126. What ailment was Threepio suffering from on the desert?

127. What area on Tatooine had been raided by sandpeople?*

128. What happened to Luke's landspeeder right after he parked it in front of the cantina?

129. What was Luke's nickname?*

130. What was Biggs's rank on the Rand Ecliptic?*

131. Where did Biggs make contact with the Rebellion?*

132. What made Uncle Owen insist that Luke postpone his application to the Academy?

133. Who were the Imperial officers mentioned in *Star Wars*, other than Darth Vader?

134. Who were the Rebels mentioned by name in *Star Wars*?

135. Who did the bartender say the cantina on Tatooine would not serve?

136. Who caused Vader to go spinning off into space in the battle of the Death Star?

137. What was Threepio willing to donate if it would help repair Artoo at the end of the movie?

138. What did Luke and Ben find in the desert that made them think Artoo and Threepio were being traced by Imperial troops?

139. How did Ben know it wasn't the work of the sandpeople?

140. Which vehicles or types of vehicles appear in *Star Wars*, but not in *Empire*?*

141. The Lars homestead was beneath
the surface of the planet.　　　　T　F

142. When the sandpeople attacked
Luke, Threepio lost his right arm.　T　F

143. Artoo stands on two legs but
"walks" on all three.　　　　　T　F

144. The sandpeople captured R2-D2
and C-3PO.　　　　　　　　T　F

145. Luke was Red 5 in *Star Wars*.　T　F

146. The creature that grabbed Luke
in the garbage compacter also got
hold of Han.　　　　　　　　T　F

147. Yoda appears in both *Star Wars* and *Empire*.　　　　T　F

148. Leia was the leader of the Rebel Alliance.　　　　T　F

149. Luke is right-handed.　　　　T　F

150. The AT-AT walkers destroyed the Rebel power generators on Hoth.　　　　T　F

151. Lobot was a bounty hunter.　　　　T　F

152. Dagobah was mainly swamp land.*　　　　T　F

153. Boba Fett's ship was gray.　　　　T　F

154. Yoda is 7′ 6″.　　　　T　F

155. Vader killed Admiral Ozzel.　　　　T　F

156. Yoda lived in the Bespin system.　　　　T　F

157. Boba Fett, IG-88, Greedo, and Bossk were the only bounty hunters to appear in the movies.* T F

158. Yoda lived in a cave. T F

159. Luke Skywalker was a commander of the Rebel Alliance. T F

160. Zev was Luke's gunner in the snowspeeder. T F

161. Luke was only partially submerged in healing fluids in the rejuvenation chamber. T F

162. Darth Vader used the mind probe to torture Han. T F

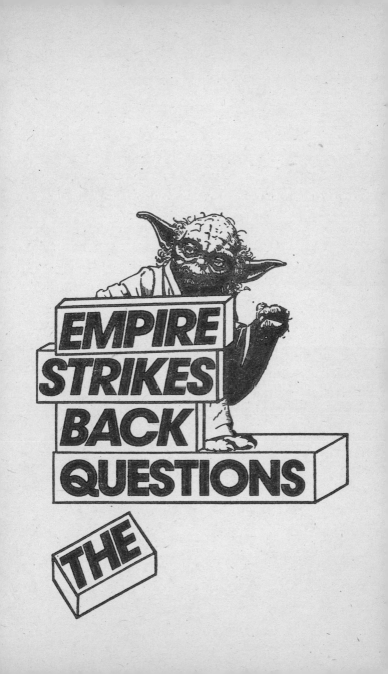

THE EMPIRE STRIKES BACK QUESTIONS

163. What ultimate plan did Vader have for Luke?

164. What was the color of Vader's hair?

165. Who was the commander of the lead walker in the Hoth snow battle?

166. How many Star Destroyers are seen in the Imperial fleet?

167. What was the surgeon droid's name?*

168. What was the surgeon droid's assistant called?*

169. What was the name of Wedge's gunner in the Hoth battle?

170. Which two characters went off in search of Han at the end of *Empire*?

171. What was the name of the ship that the Rebels used to evacuate Hoth?

172. What planet did Yoda live on?

173. What creature was the Millennium Falcon hidden inside of in the asteroid belt?*

174. What substance was Han Solo frozen in?

175. Which of the bounty hunters captured Han?

176. What creatures attacked the Falcon when it was inside the space slug?

177. What Rebel vehicles were used to battle the AT-AT walkers?

178. What weapon was used to clear the way for the Rebel transports leaving Hoth?

179. What system did Lando Calrissian live in?

180. What protected the Hoth base from aerial bombardment?

181. Why did Vader kill Admiral Ozzel?

182. Who did Vader promote to Admiral Ozzel's position?

183. How many AT-AT walkers did the Rebel troops see on the north ridge advancing on the Hoth base?

184. What equipment did the Rebels use to bring down the AT-AT walker?

185. Who informed Vader that the Emperor demanded contact with him?

186. What did Yoda cook for Luke?

187. Who did Darth Vader kill for allowing the Falcon to escape after leaving the asteroid field?

188. What was Lando's position in Cloud City?

189. Who described the Falcon as the "fastest hunk of junk in the galaxy"?

190. What creatures did the Rebels ride on Hoth?

191. What creature attacked Luke on Hoth?

192. What healing substance was Luke submerged in?

193. What part of Luke's body did Darth Vader sever?

194. What did Luke do to free himself from the ice in the Wampa's cave?

195. What was the primary industry of Cloud City?

196. Who was the previous owner of the Millennium Falcon?

197. What mechanical failure kept the Falcon from going into hyperspace?

198. Who was Luke's gunner in the snow battle on Hoth?

199. How many times and where did Ben Kenobi materialize when he spoke to Luke?

200. What fate did Vader initially plan for Leia and Chewbacca on Bespin, and how did he alter it later?

201. Why did Luke remain outside on the plains of Hoth when Han went back to the base?

202. Why did Han go out to rescue Luke on a Tauntaun instead of a snowspeeder?

203. Which Star Destroyer was under Captain Needa's command?*

204. How did Luke ultimately escape from Darth Vader in the lightsaber duel?

205. What was the name of Boba Fett's spaceship?*

206. What relationship did Darth Vader claim to have with Luke Skywalker?

207. What was Darth Vader's Star Destroyer called?*

208. What was Boba Fett planning to do with Han Solo?

209. Who was Lando Calrissian's personal aide?

210. What was Chewbacca's mistake in reconstructing Threepio?

211. What course did the Falcon take entering the asteroid field and who set it?

212. How often did the Falcon's crew try to engage the hyperdrive and fail and during which scenes?

213. What were the approximate odds of surviving a trip through an asteroid field, according to Threepio?

214. What components did Han check on the Falcon the first time the hyperdrive failed?

215. Who claimed "It's not my fault," and when?

216. Who is referred to as "The Professor"?

217. When the Falcon's crew floated away with the Star Destroyer's garbage, what system was the ship in?

218. How was the Imperial Probot destroyed on Hoth?

219. Who distracted the Probot so it could be destroyed?

220. How many "legs" did the Probot have?

221. What kind of droid was IG-88?*

222. Which general commanded the Hoth base?

223. What code word did Lando use to make the Cloud City guards capture the Imperial stormtroopers?

224. Where was Vader when he was seen without his helmet?

225. What did Han use to cut open the dead Tauntaun?

226. What vehicles were used to patrol the outside of Cloud City?*

227. Who called Han a pirate?

228. What did Artoo say were the odds against Luke and Han's survival on the plains of Hoth?

229. What was another name used to refer to the Hoth Base?

230. What sector of the Rebel base and in what direction was the Probot moving in?

231. How many forms of communication was Threepio familiar with?

232. What sector of the Rebel base on Hoth did the Imperial fleet come out of hyperspace in?

233. Who were the Imperials mentioned in *Empire* besides Darth Vader?

234. Who were the Rebels mentioned in *Empire*?

235. What entrance were the troop carriers assembled at for the evacuation of Hoth?

236. What was Luke's code name during the battle on Hoth?

237. What was the attack pattern Luke and Dack used?

238. What was the evacuation code signal for the troops on Hoth?

239. What piece of machinery was Luke holding onto at the bottom of Cloud City?*

240. What two tools did Han use to repair the Falcon?

241. How did Han come to possess the Millennium Falcon?

242. Who made the first successful shot at an AT-AT walker with a harpoon?

243. Who is referred to as a type of flower?

244. Where did the Falcon hide from the Imperial fleet after it emerged from the mouth of the space slug?

245. Where did the lightsaber duel between Luke and Darth Vader end?

246. Which character finally repaired the Falcon's hyperdrive at the end of *Empire*?

247. What part of the Falcon was Chewbacca working on at the beginning of *Empire*?*

248. How did R2-D2 get free from the swamp monster on Dagobah?

249. What was R2-D2 doing to try to locate Han and Luke in the snowstorm on Hoth?*

250. What was the main objective of the AT-AT walkers?

251. Who were Zuckuss and Dengar?*

252. Where was Boba Fett's ship docked in Cloud City?

253. Where was the Millennium Falcon docked in Cloud City?*

254. What was the two-legged walker called?*

255. Where did Vader and Luke start their duel?

256. What was the color of the snowspeeders?

257. What kind of creature is a Tauntaun?*

258. What color were the flying vehicles used to guard Cloud City?

259. Why was Darth Vader at Cloud City?

260. How many horns did a Tauntaun have?

261. What creatures formed the work force in Cloud City?

262. Whose code name was Rogue Three in the snowspeeder group on Hoth?

263. Who was Echo 7?

264. What kind of stick did Yoda carry?

265. Who did Leia fall in love with?

266. What color was an Ugnaught's worksuit?

267. What color was an Ugnaught's smock?

268. What color was a Bespin guard's uniform and hat?

269. What ships besides the Falcon were seen in the Rebel ice hangar?

270. Where was Cloud City?

271. How did Admiral Piett die?

272. How did the medical droid Too-Onebee solve the problem of Luke's amputated hand?

273. What did Han do to Lando when the administrator tried to excuse his treachery?

274. What happened to the Star Destroyer the Rebels shot with the ion cannon?*

275. What did the other 3PO unit say to C-3PO in the corridor of Cloud City?*

276. What did Vader use besides his lightsaber in his duel with Luke?

277. What made radar detection from Hoth very difficult?*

278. What optical instrument was used by Rebel officers on Hoth?*

279. What was the color of a Tauntaun?

280. What color were the eyes of a Wampa Ice Creature?

281. What was the walkie-talkie-like mode of communication used by the Rebels on Hoth?

282. What was the radar-like scanning device used by the Empire?*

283. What does AT-AT stand for?*

284. How was Luke able to understand the language used by R2-D2 when they were in the X-wing fighter?*

285. Who was the only person to see Vader without his helmet?

286. What object did Yoda take from Luke's supply case?

287. Who was the bounty hunter in ESB with a soft, baggy face and bloodshot eyes?*

288. What did Lando claim to have won in a sabacc match?*

289. What did the Avenger release before zooming into hyperspace?*

290. Who did Luke think he encountered inside the tree?

291. What kept Cloud City suspended over Bespin?*

292. What color were the structures in Cloud City's business and residential sections?*

293. How was Threepio damaged in Cloud City?

294. What vision of the future did Luke see using the Force under Yoda's guidance?

295. Where did Chewbacca find the dismembered Threepio in Cloud City?*

296. Why was Lando afraid of the Empire?

297. What deal had Lando made to protect himself from the Empire?

298. What was Luke and Artoo's first inkling that something was wrong when they arrived in Cloud City?*

299. Which vehicles or types of vehicles appear only in *Empire*?*

QUESTIONS
FROM
BOTH
MOVIES

300. Who was the only Rebel fighter pilot besides Luke to appear in both movies?

301. What wars did Ben Kenobi fight in long ago?

302. What rank did he hold?

303. What kind of droid was Threepio?

304. What was the name of the governing system before the Empire took over?

305. What was the color of Darth Vader's lightsaber blade?

306. What were the three uses of the Imperial Star Destroyer's bottom hatch?

307. What does the TIE in TIE fighter stand for?*

308. Where did Darth Vader wear his lightsaber?

309. What were a droid's mechanical eyes called?*

310. What kind of creature was Chewbacca?

311. How many guns did an X-wing fighter have?

312. How many engines were on a Star Destroyer?

313. How many pilots did a Y-wing fighter accommodate?

314. How many pilots did an X-wing fighter accommodate?

315. What were the colors of the Rebel pilots' flight suits in *Star Wars* and *The Empire Strikes Back*?

316. What was the color of R2-D2's trim?

317. What mechanical function did a power droid have?*

318. What was Darth Vader's full title?*

319. What did Imperial officers call Vader?

320. How many photoreceptors did R2-D2 have?

321. What was the Emperor's name?*

322. What is another term for hyperspace?

323. What were Chewbacca's duties?

324. Whom was Han Solo in debt to?

325. What were the eight ways Han addressed the Princess?

326. Who said "I have a bad feeling about this," and when?

327. What were the names of the planets or systems mentioned or visited in both movies?

328. Which vehicles or types of vehicles appear in both movies?

329. What creature did Ben fend off from Luke in the cantina?*

330. What creature pulled Luke under the muck in the trash compacter?*

331. What was the code number of the trash compacter?

332. What kind of creature did the stormtroopers ride on Tatooine, while looking for R2-D2 and C-3PO?*

333. What small droid was scared by Chewbacca on the Death Star?*

334. How many holographic creatures were used in the game Chewie and the droids played on the Falcon?

335. What were the wings on an X-wing fighter called?

336. What was the new model of landspeeder that made Luke's less valuable?

337. Who was Red 6 in the battle of the Death Star?

338. What are the titles of the sixteen musical segments written for *Star Wars*?*

339. What are the titles of the seventeen musical segments written for *The Empire Strikes Back*?*

340. Who was Red 2?

341. Who called Luke "the best bush pilot in the outer rim territories"?*

342. How did Lt. Porkins die in the battle of the Death Star?*

343. What was the code name for the storm-trooper who left his post while guarding the Millennium Falcon on the Death Star?

344. What was the name of the farming community where Luke visited his friends Deak, Windy, and Biggs?*

345. What caused a landspeeder to float?*

346. What was the name of Chewbacca's home planet?*

347. When is Anthony Daniels' birthday?*

348. When is Sir Alec Guinness's birthday?*

349. When is Peter Mayhew's birthday?*

350. When is David Prowse's birthday?*

351. When is Harrison Ford's birthday?*

352. When is Kenny Baker's birthday?*

353. When is Mark Hamill's birthday?*

354. When is Carrie Fisher's birthday?*

355. When is Billy Dee Williams's birthday?*

356. When is Irvin Kershner's birthday?*

357. What was the enemy force in *Han Solo at Stars' End*?*

358. What was Artoo's robot classification?*

359. What was Leia Organa's signet of office?*

360. What weapons were in the knees of Boba Fett's suit?*

361. Who was the snowspeeder pilot who crashed into the lead walker?*

362. What defensive equipment did the Probot have?*

363. Which pilot rescued Luke and Han on Hoth?*

364. Who played the Rebel soldiers who were manning the ground emplacements on Hoth?*

365. How did General Veers die?*

BEHIND THE SCENES QUESTIONS

366. Where was the Yavin base filmed?*

367. Where was Tatooine filmed?*

368. Who directed *Star Wars*?

369. What is the only book in which a script of *Star Wars* is available?*

370. What record company distributed the soundtrack for *Star Wars*?

371. What was the title of George Lucas's first full-length movie?*

372. Who did most of the preliminary sketches for *Star Wars*?

373. Who was the chief model builder for *Star Wars*?

374. Who was the costume designer for *Star Wars*?

375. Who were the film editors for *Star Wars*?

376. Who was the first cameraman in the miniature and optical effects unit for *Star Wars*?

377. The *Star Wars* saga is told from which two characters' points of view, according to George Lucas?*

378. What will the third *Star Wars* movie be called?*

379. Who produced *Star Wars* and *The Empire Strikes Back*?

380. What is the name of the facility where the special effects were created for *Star Wars* and *Empire*?*

381. What is bluescreen?*

382. What orchestra performed the music for *Star Wars* and *The Empire Strikes Back*?*

383. What were the three Han Solo books published by Ballantine?

384. What company publishes *Star Wars* comics?

385. Who published the *Star Wars* and *The Empire Strikes Back Storybooks*?

386. Who composed the scores for *Star Wars* and *Empire*?*

387. What day did filming of *Revenge of the Jedi* begin?*

388. Where were the Hoth scenes filmed?

389. Who directed *The Empire Strikes Back*?

390. Which two artists made most of the *Empire* storyboards?*

391. What kind of snakes were used on the Dagobah set?*

392. What two people wrote the *Empire* screenplay?

393. Was the Probot filmed with a miniature or a full-size model, or both?*

394. What natural disaster caused the camera crew to be delayed in Norway?*

395. When did principal photography on *Empire* begin?*

396. What was the release date for *Empire*?*

397. What record company distributed the sound-track for *Empire*?*

398. Who did the disco rendition of *The Empire Strikes Back* and the "Force" theme?*

399. Who wrote the novel, *The Empire Strikes Back*?*

400. Where was the soundtrack for *ESB* recorded?

401. When Ben Kenobi warned Luke about Mos Eisley, he described the place as ———— (fill in the blank).

402. What did Han say to the bartender in the cantina when he paid him?

403. What curse did Threepio make when he thought his friends were dying in the trash compacter?

404. What were Ben Kenobi's first words to Luke after being killed by Darth Vader?

405. What warning did Ben Kenobi give Darth Vader during the lightsaber duel?

✦✦✦✦✦✦✦✦✦✦✦✦✦✦✦✦✦✦✦✦✦✦✦✦✦✦✦✦✦✦✦

406. What excuse did Luke, Han, and Chewie use to get into the Death Star detention area?

407. What was Tarkin's retort when his aide suggested escaping in his personal ship?

408. What did the bartender in the cantina say as Luke and Ben were confronting the aliens?

409. What did Leia tell Luke when Han left before the battle of the Death Star?

410. What did Han say to Luke just after the Death Star exploded?

411. What is the famous opening phrase of both *Star Wars* and *Empire*?

412. What was Han's boast to Luke and Ben in the cantina about the Falcon's speed?

✦✦✦✦✦✦✦✦✦✦✦✦✦✦✦✦✦✦✦✦✦✦✦✦✦✦✦✦✦✦✦

413. What did Han tell Luke after Luke's recovery from the Wampa attack? "You look strong enough to ———."

414. What did Yoda call the place where he sent Luke to learn about the dark side of the Force?

415. What 4-part name did Leia give Han?

416. What were Lando's first words to Han?

417. What did Yoda tell Luke about adventure?

418. What was Han's comment to himself when he cut open the dead Tauntaun?

419. What three words did Yoda use to describe the dark side of the Force?

420. How did Han describe Lando to Leia?

421. What did Yoda tell Luke was inside the tree?

422. What were Luke's first words after he was rescued by the Falcon?

423. What were the last words Luke said to Lando and Chewie as they departed?

424. Name the actors who played the following:

Chewbacca

Princess Leia Organa

Ben (Obi-Wan) Kenobi

Darth Vader

Han Solo

Luke Skywalker

R2-D2 (Artoo-Detoo)

C-3PO (See-Threepio)

Grand Moff Tarkin

Boba Fett

Yoda

Lando Calrissian

425. Match the actors (on the left) with the roles they played (on the right).

William Hootkins   General Rieekan

Richard Le Parmentier   Wedge Antilles

Jack Purvis   General Dodonna

John Morton   Lobot

Dennis Lawson   Chief Ugnaught

Bruce Boa   General Motti

Shelagh Fraser   Admiral Piett

Garrick Hagon   Wampa Ice Creature

Don Henderson   General Veers

Des Webb   Dak

Phil Brown   Aunt Beru

Michael Sheard   General Tagge

Kenneth Colley   Porkins

Julian Glover   Admiral Ozzel

Alex McCrindle   Biggs

John Hollis   Chief Jawa

Eddie Byrne   General Willard

                         Uncle Owen

◆ ANSWERS ◆
STAR WARS

1. Mos Eisley.

2. Alderaan.

3. Greedo.

4. A landspeeder.

5. A sandcrawler.

6. Blockade Runner.

7. Biggs and Tank.

8. Rand Ecliptic.

9. A small thermal exhaust port.

10. He gave a krayt dragon call.

11. They would be sent to the spice mines of Kessel or smashed into who-knows-what.

12. In an escape pod.

13. It might generate sympathy for the Rebellion in the Imperial Senate.

14. He had a distress signal sent from the Blockade Runner and then reported that all aboard were killed.

15. His red light goes on.

16. Their tracks and a small metal ring.

17. A model ship (in the novel: a T-16 skyhopper).

18. To the south ridge to work on the condensers.

19. Moisture farming.

20. Moisture vaporators.

21. Banthas.

22. To be in the Academy.

23. Tatoo I and Tatoo II.

24. General Willard.

25. The jawas.

26. Alderaan.

27. Darth Vader.

28. Motti.

29. He had an elephant's trunk for a nose.

30. .5 past lightspeed.

31. A helmet with its blast shield down.

32. Dantooine.

33. Six.

34. A diplomatic mission.

35. Four.

36. Because an Imperial ship boarded the Falcon, and Han dumped a load of spice belonging to Jabba.

37. Nine.

38. A Gaderffii stick.

39. From the belt on his stormtrooper uniform.

40. It had curved (or angular) wings.

41. The escape pod registered no life forms.

42. A mind probe.

43. His macrobinoculars.

44. Melt them down.

45. To have Artoo's memory erased.

46. Three.

47. Motti.

48. Tarkin.

49. They burned them.

50. Two.

51. He cut in the sublight engines.

52. They chased a TIE fighter.

53. Four.

54. Docking Bay 94.

55. The technical readouts from the Death Star.

56. Beyond the Dune Sea.

57.   Darth Vader.

58.   Imperial stormtroopers.

59.   R5-D4.

60.   Tarkin's.

61.   Remote.

62.   In the trash compacter.

63.   His cloak and lightsaber.

64.   He thought the Rebellion would be ended.

65.   Governor. He was also called "Grand Moff Tarkin."

66.   Biggs.

67.   Lt. Porkins.

68.   Red and gold (in the novel, blue and gold).

69. The T-16 Skyhopper.

70. It could destroy planets.

71. Red Leader (in the novel, Blue Leader and Blue Ten).

72. To repair a small hit, lock down a stabilizer that breaks loose, and increase the ship's power.

73. General Dodonna.

74. Artoo plugged into a computer outlet.

75. They put a homing beacon on the ship.

76. Bullseye-ing womp-rats on Tatooine.

77. He fired his blaster, which ricocheted.

78. On the fourth moon of Yavin.

79. A tractor beam.

80. Stormtrooper armor.

81. Four.

82. Luke Skywalker.

83. Through a vacuum tube.

84. AA-23.

85. Several transmissions were beamed to the ship by Rebel spies.

86. Programming binary load lifters.

87. It had a bad motivator.

88. The Maker.

89. He found carbon scoring on Artoo.

90. The restraining bolt.

91. Uncle Owen.

92. That he had been a navigator on a spice freighter.

93. Round.

94. The local governors.

95. He tapped it with his foot.

96. Toshi Station.

97. He was in the Death Star when it exploded.

98. The Imperial starfleet.

99. The Death Star defense systems.

100. Bail Antilles.

101. They were killed by stormtroopers.

102. They absorb moisture from the atmosphere.

103. Ben Kenobi, who got it from Luke's father.

104. Her father.

105. The navi-computer.

106. The log said the crew had abandoned ship, and the escape pods had been jettisoned.

107. Seven.

108. To destroy it.

109. To disengage the tractor beam.

110. A mindless philosopher.

111. General Dodonna.

112. She shot one and was then knocked unconscious by a stun blast.

113. Hold his gun.

114. As greater than half that of the Imperial fleet.

115. Thirty.

116. Lars.

117. Bocce.

118. In a hologram.

119. The Jundland Wastes.

120. Viceroy and First Chairman of the Alderaan System.

121. Seventeen thousand: two in advance and fifteen when Han reached Alderaan.

122. The remains of a Rebel base.

123. 2187.

124. Proton torpedoes.

125. At the cantina in Mos Eisley.

126. Semifrozen joints.

127. The outskirts of Anchorhead.

128. A jawa scurried up and began fondling it.

129. Wormie.

130. First mate.

131. Bestine.

132. He needed him on the farm for another season.

133. Tarkin, Motti, and Tagge.

134. Captain Antilles, Dodonna, Willard, Wedge, Biggs, Tiree, Dutch, Porkins, Princess Leia, Luke Skywalker, Obi-Wan Kenobi, and John D.

135. Droids.

136. Han Solo.

137. Circuits or gears.

138. An obliterated sandcrawler.

139. The Bantha tracks were side by side instead of single file, and the blaster marks were too accurate.

140. Sandcrawler, escape pod, landspeeder, Vader's TIE fighter, Blockade Runner, and various Mos Eisley vehicles.

♦ ANSWERS ♦
TRUE / FALSE

141. True.

142. True.

143. True.

144. False.

145. True (in the novel, Blue 5).

146. False.

147. False.

148. True.

149. True.

150. True.

151. False.

152. True.

153. False.

154. False.

155. True.

156. False.

157. False.

158. False.

159. True.

160. False.

161. False.

162. False.

163. To take over Luke's training so that the two of them could rule the Empire together.

164. He didn't have any.

165. General Veers.

166. Six.

167. Too-Onebee.

168. FX-7.

169. Janson.

170. Chewie and Lando.

171. The Rebel Transport.

172. Dagobah.

173. A space slug.

174. Carbonite.

175. Boba Fett.

176. Mynocks.

177. Snowspeeders.

178. The ion cannon.

179. Bespin.

180. An energy field.

181. He had the Starfleet come out of lightspeed too close to the Hoth system.

182. Captain Piett.

183.   Five.

184.   A harpoon with a tow cable attached to it.

185.   Admiral Piett.

186.   Rootleaf.

187.   Captain Needa.

188.   Administrator.

189.   Lando.

190.   Tauntauns.

191.   A Wampa Ice Creature.

192.   Bacta.

193.   His hand.

194.   He used the Force to get his lightsaber and
       cut himself down.

195. Tibanna gas mining.

196. Lando Calrissian.

197. The hyperdrive motivator was damaged. (In the novel they called it the para-light system.)

198. Dak (or Dack).

199. Twice: once on Hoth, once on Dagobah.

200. He said they must never leave Cloud City, and then decided to take them on his ship as prisoners.

201. Luke wanted to check a meteorite that fell nearby.

202. The Rebel mechanics were having trouble adapting the snowspeeders to the cold.

203. The *Avenger*.

204. By jumping into an exhaust shaft.

205. *Slave I.*

206. He said he was Luke's father.

207. The *Executor.*

208. Take him to Jabba the Hutt to collect his bounty.

209. Lobot.

210. He put Threepio's head on backward.

211. Chewie set course 271.

212. Three times: Fleeing Hoth, leaving the asteroid field, and leaving Cloud City.

213. 3720:1.

214. The horizontal boosters and alluvial dampers.

215. Han and Lando, when each attempts to engage the hyperdrive and fails.

216. Threepio.

217. The Anoat system.

218. Han shot it.

219. Chewbacca.

220. Five.

221. A chrome war droid.

222. General Rieekan.

223. Code-Force-Seven.

224. In the meditation chamber.

225. Luke's lightsaber.

226. Twin-pod cloud cars.

227. Lando.

228. 725:1.

THE JEDI MASTER'S QUIZBOOK

229. Echo Base.

230. Zone 12 moving east.

231. Six million.

232. Sector 4.

233. Piett, Ozzel, Veers, and Needa.

234. Rieekan, Derlin, Zev, Dak, Hobbie, Wedge, Janson, Princess Leia, Luke.

235. At the North Entrance.

236. Rogue Leader.

237. Delta.

238. K-one-zero.

239. A weather vane.

240. Fusion cutter and hydrospanners.

241. He won it from Lando.

242. Janson.

243. Threepio (Goldenrod).

244. It clung to the top of Captain Needa's Star Destroyer, the *Avenger*.

245. On the gantry that extends out into the reactor shaft.

246. R2-D2.

247. The central lifters.

248. It spit him out.

249. Using his built-in probe sensors to try to pick up evidence of either Luke or Han.

250. To destroy the Rebel power generator.

251. Bounty hunters.

252. On the East platform.

253. Landing Platform 327.

254. The scout walker.

255. Above the carbon-freezing chamber.

256. Gray, with rust-colored trim.

257. A Hoth snow lizard.

258. Orange.

259. To try to capture Luke.

260. Two.

261. The Ugnaughts.

262. Wedge.

263. Han Solo.

264. Gimer stick.

265. Han.

266. Gray.

267. Blue.

268. Dark blue with gold trim.

269. Snowspeeders and X-wing fighters.

270. Above the planet Bespin.

271. He didn't.

272. He built a bionic hand in place of the old one.

273. He punched Lando.

274. Its conning tower was damaged, and it spun out of control (novel).

275. "E chu Ta!"

276. He used the Force to hurl machinery at Luke.

277. Meteorite activity.

278. Electrobinoculars.

279. Gray or gray spotted.

280. Brownish.

281. The comlink.

282. Com-Scan.

283. All Terrain Armored Transport.

284. A miniature computer translated for him.

285. General Veers. (In the novel: Admiral Piett.)

286. A tiny power lamp.

287. Bossk.

288. The mining colony of Cloud City.

289. Garbage and sections of irreparable machinery.

290. Darth Vader.

291. A thin unipod, surrounded at the base by a large, round reactor.

292. White.

293. He was shot and dismembered.

294. Cloud City and his friends in pain.

295. In the junk room.

296. The Empire had the power to shut down his mining operation.

297. He agreed to turn Han and his friends over to Boba Fett and Vader.

298. No one asked to see their identification or landing permit.

299. AT-AT walkers, Twin-pod cloud cars, Rebel Star Cruiser, Rebel Transport, Slave I, snow-speeders, TIE bombers.

◆ ANSWERS ◆
BOTH MOVIES

300. Wedge.

301. The Clone Wars.

302. General.

303. A human-droid relations specialist, or protocol droid.

304. The Old Republic.

305. Red.

306. It captured ships, dumped garbage, and deployed Probots.

307. Twin Ion Engine.

308. Clipped to his belt.

309. Photoreceptors.

310. A Wookiee.

311. Four.

312. Three.

313. Two.

314. One pilot and a droid.

315. Orange (with some white and gray).

316. Blue.

317. "Juicing up" other droids.

318. Darth Vader, Lord of the Sith.

319. Lord Vader.

320. One.

321. Palpatine.

322. Lightspeed.

323. He was copilot on the Falcon and chief mechanic.

324. Jabba the Hutt.

325. Leia, Your Highness, Sweetheart, Your Worship, Your Worshipfulness, Sister, Your Highnessness, and Princess.

326. Luke, when the Falcon approached the Death Star. Leia, when she was walking around the inside of the space slug. Han, when the walls of the trash compacter started to move in.

327. Kessel, Tatooine, Alderaan, Dantooine, Yavin, Dagobah, Bespin, Ord Mantell, Anoat,
and Hoth.

328. X-wing fighters, Y-wing fighters, Millennium
Falcon, Star Destroyers, TIE fighters.

329. Snaggletooth.

330. The Dianoga.

331. 3263827.

332. A Patrol Dewback.

333. The mouse robot.

334. Eight.

335. S-foils.

336. The XP-38.

337. Porkins. (In the novel he was Blue Four.)

338. "Main Title," "Imperial Attack," "Princess Leia's Theme," "The Desert and the Robot Auction," "The Land of the Sandpeople," "Mouse Robot and Blasting Off," "The Return Home," "The Walls Converge," "The Princess Appears," "Ben's Death and the TIE Fighter Attack," "The Little People Work," "Rescue of the Princess," "Inner City," "Cantina Band," "The Last Battle," "The Throne Room," and "End Title."

339. "Star Wars" (main theme), "Yoda's Theme," "The Training of a Jedi Knight," "The Heroics of Luke and Han," "The Imperial March" (Darth Vader's Theme), "Departure of Boba Fett," "Han Solo and the Princess," "Hyperspace," "The Battle in the Snow," "The Asteroid Field," "The City in the Clouds," "Rebels at Bay," "Yoda and the Force," "The Duel," "The Magic Tree," "Lando's Palace," and "Finale."

340. Wedge (Blue 2 in the novel).

341. Biggs.

342. His fighter was destroyed by Vader's ship when his instrument panel malfunctioned (novel only).

343. TK-421. (THX-1138 in the novel.)

344. Anchorhead.

345. A magnetic field.

346. Kashyyyk.

347. February 21.

348. April 2.

349. May 19.

350. July 1.

351. July 13.

352. August 24.

353. September 25.

354. October 21.

355. April 6.

356. April 27.

357. The corporate sector authority.

358. Thermocapsulary dehousing assister (also astro-droid).

359. Chalcedony waves.

360. Rocket darts.

361. Hobbie (but in the movie he didn't crash).

362. It could generate a protective force field (novel).

363. Rogue Two (Zev).

364. The Norwegian Red Cross Rescue Skiers.

365. His walker was destroyed when a snowspeeder flew through the windscreen (novel
only).

366. Guatemala.

367. Tunisia.

368. George Lucas.

369. *The Art of Star Wars.*

370. 20th Century Records.

371. THX-1138.

372. Ralph McQuarrie.

373. Grant McCune.

374. John Mollo.

375. Paul Hirsch, Marcia Lucas, and Richard Chew.

376. Richard Edlund.

377. R2-D2 and C-3PO.

378. *Revenge of the Jedi.*

379. Gary Kurtz.

380. Industrial Light and Magic.

381. The process that enables live action and models to be filmed together in *Star Wars* and *Empire.*

382. The London Symphony Orchestra.

383. *Han Solo at Stars' End, Han Solo's Revenge, Han Solo and the Lost Legacy.*

384. Marvel Comics.

385. Random House.

386. John Williams.

387. Jan. 11, 1982.

388. Finse, Norway.

389. Irvin Kershner.

390. Joe Johnston and Nilo Rodis-Jamero.

391. King snakes and boa constrictors.

392. Leigh Brackett and Lawrence Kasdan.

393. Both.

394. An avalanche.

395. March 5, 1979.

396. May 21, 1980.

397. RSO Records.

398. Meco.

399. Donald F. Glut.

400. Anvil Recording Studios in Denham, England.

401. "A . . . wretched hive of scum and villainy."

402. "Sorry about the mess."

403. "Curse my metal body!"

404. "Run, Luke, run."

405. "If you strike me down, I shall become more powerful than you can possibly imagine."

406. "Prisoner transfer from Cell Block 1138."

407. "Evacuate? In our moment of triumph? I think you overestimate their chances."

408. "No blasters. No blasters."

409. "He's got to follow his own path. No one can choose it for him."

410. "Great shot, kid. That was one in a million!"

411. "A long time ago in a galaxy far, far away . . ."

412. "It's the ship that made the Kessel run in less than twelve parsecs."

413. "Pull the ears off a Gundark."

414. "A domain of evil."

415. "You stuck-up, half-witted, scruffy-looking nerf-herder."

416. "Why you slimy, double-crossing, no-good swindler. You've got a lot of guts coming here, after what you pulled."

417. "Adventure . . . excitement . . . a Jedi craves not these things."

418. "I thought they smelled bad on the *outside!*"

419. "Anger, fear, aggression."

420. "He's a card-player, gambler, scoundrel."

421. "Only what you take with you."

422. "Oh, Leia."

423. "Take care, you two, may the Force be with you."

424. Chewbacca—Peter Mayhew
Princess Leia—Carrie Fisher
Ben Kenobi—Sir Alec Guinness
Darth Vader—David Prowse (Voice: James
    Earl Jones)
Han Solo—Harrison Ford
Luke Skywalker—Mark Hamill
R2-D2—Kenny Baker
C-3PO—Anthony Daniels
Grand Moff Tarkin—Peter Cushing
Boba Fett—Jeremy Bulloch
Yoda—Frank Oz (Yoda's puppeteer)
Lando Calrissian—Billy Dee Williams

◆ ANSWERS ◆
MATCH
THE ACTORS

425. William Hootkins—Porkins; Richard Le Parmentier—Admiral Motti; Jack Purvis—Chief Ugnaught and Chief Jawa; John Morton—Dak; Dennis Lawson—Wedge Antilles; Bruce Boa—General Rieekan; Shelagh Fraser—Aunt Beru; Garrick Hagon—Biggs; Don Henderson—General Tagge; Des Webb—Wampa Ice Creature; Phil Brown—Uncle Owen; Michael Sheard—Admiral Ozzel; Kenneth Colley—Admiral Piett; Julian Glover—General Veers; Alex McCrindle—General Dodonna; John Hollis—Lobot; Eddie Byrne—General Willard.

ABOUT THE AUTHOR

Rusty Miller has red hair, lots of freckles, wears braces and smiles a lot—he's an all-American kid.

Rusty takes guitar lessons, sings in the school chorus and is an A student enrolled in The Gifted Students' Program.

He lives in Florida with his parents and maintains that his "best friend" is his dachshund, Frodo.

This is Rusty's first book.